Tales of My Little Whatevers

Alexandria Lu

BookLeaf Publishing

India | USA | UK

Tales of My Little Whatevers © 2023
Alexandria Lu

Presentation by *BookLeaf Publishing*

Web: www.bookleafpub.com

E-mail: info@bookleafpub.com

ISBN: 9789357690157

First edition 2023

I dedicate this book to my sister in faith and in writing.

ACKNOWLEDGEMENT

I'd like to thank my beautiful mother for inspiring me in more ways than one, and helping me along this journey. You have encouraged me to step out of my norm and do something I was too afraid of. Thank you for being with me every step of the way, and helping me through this process. My heart carries deep love for you.

Dream Wasteland

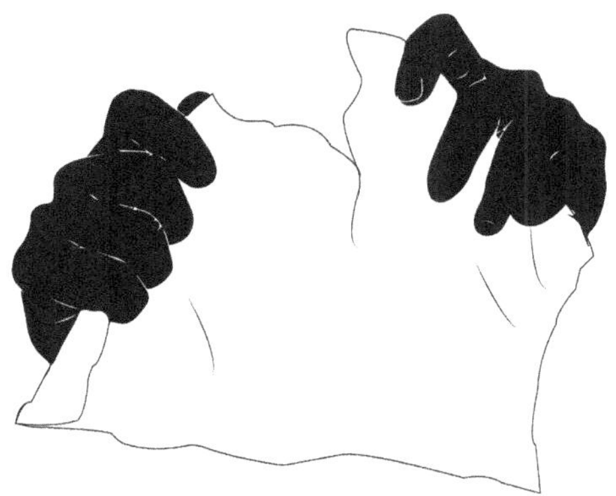

It Wasn't supposed to be like this,
Adventureless adventures,
Traveling through times end,
Not really seeing the things promised,
Numbfully feeling feelings I'm not even sure
exist

When will the prime of my life be?
I was told it was now,
But then again they lied about everything else

Maybe life is really just a lottery,
And only few get to live it,
The privileged continue to recite the same
empty speeches,
'Your day is coming just look at me',

I adjust my eyes and still all I see,
False prophets scattered all around me,

Do not let your spirits die,
Who knows maybe one day it will be you,
But when will one day be?
Perhaps the thirty-fifth of next month,
I guess I have to just wait and see

I'm starting to suspect hope is only for the
young,
For the older I get the less it seems to matter,
The ones who told me to hold on tight to the
things that I dream,
Now tell me at my age I have to give them up
But now I've decided to die on this hill,
For now I'm just delusional,
Humming a tuneless song.

The Flowerless Garden

For how long must I water a flowerless garden,
It seems as if decades have passed,
Yet not a single rose

I cry out and I scream,
Yet all I get is silence,
I quake and I quiver,
Yet not a single touch

Just when I gain the courage to give in to my
insanity,
A bouquet of promises breaks through my
window,

But alas,
Every promise that's promised is a promise
that's broken;

I wonder if promises go numb just like my heart
has?
Or do they simply just fade into nothingness
when not kept,
I suppose that's a mystery that was never meant
to be solved

Either way it goes,
The current has become stronger,
Pulling me to limits I do not wish to cross,
I'm drowning in waves of inconsideration,
And I cannot tell my tears apart from the torrent

How Ironic is it,
That integrity keeps me anchored,
And love keeps me sound,
Though no love is given,
And integrity cannot be found

Oh but what a horrid crime it is!
To promise a promise that one never intended to
give!
Oh what a horrid crime it is!
To break a heart that one has no intention to
mend!

No Love Lost

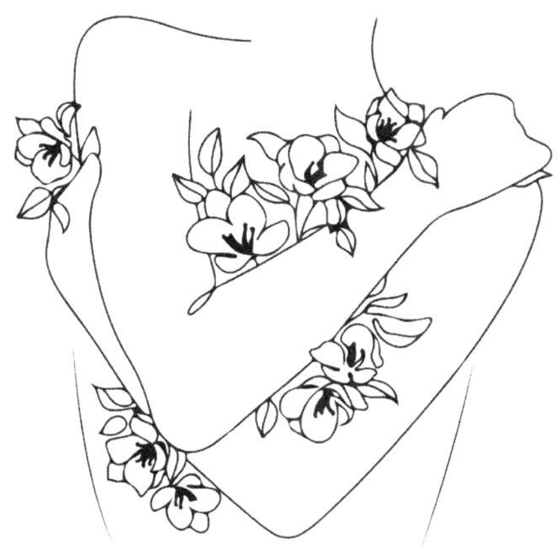

I believe in other loves,
I dance and tangle with all other forms,
I trust and believe in the love that lives and is
there for me...

God's love,
My mother's love,
What more can I need?

So why is the one that does not exist,
Constantly parading around me in all of its
ignorance?

It whispers promises that are constantly broken,
It hums a tune that is never complete,

Yet everyone in the audience eats it up, hanging
on the edge of their seats,
waiting for the release,

The release will never come...

I've been happier without and will continue to
be,
So please don't push this lying, empty, heartless
love onto me.

Smoke and Mirrors

From the outside it looked so appealing
It handed out counterfeit invitations with
promises so pleasing
It drank our tears and grew intoxicated from its
own teasing

It beautifully sang meaningless songs
And boastfully displayed to us the feast of riches
Hiding behind its glass walls,
It would show us its splendor
We were tortured by delightful aromas
Night and day we would hide from the reflection
of our own tears!
For it was only a reminder of what society said
we were…
Nothing;

Then one day I fell content
Happy with the present tense
No one knew but I got a glimpse
Inside the glass walls of excellence
Upon entrance I found nothingness
Not one word spoken meant something
Not one glance given bared a soul
Plastic hearts surrounded me

The feast and the splendor were covered in mold
You see from the outside it looked so pretty,
Only because we were not in
We couldn't see the projectors and lights
What seemed like weighted gold was hollow and
thin
Yes from the outside it looked so different,
But I guess that's why they say make the best of
where you're at
Jealousy is just an offspring of ignorance
Because you can never be jealous when you
have all of the facts.

Between Two Roads

To choose between two separate roads,
One less taken and one overflowed,
To choose between my mind and heart,
One can save me while the other cannot;

I've known a life less empty,
Though it came with pains and distress,
I've known a life so hollow,
That one fooled many with its beauty and
success;

To whose standards shall I live by?
To which one shall I fall a slave?
For the one that is empty is easy,
But the one that gives me life brings pain;

I fear that the empty road has secrets soon to be
uncovered,
For though the glamour from the outside seems
appealing,
There's no beauty on the inside that has been
discovered;

So I'll take my pains with the road less taken,
Building my roots in this road that many have
forsaken,
For my reward surely must outweigh my
troubles,
I've gained contentment with my decision,
Because whatever my reward is, I know it will
be double.

When Leaves Drift

We drifted apart like two leaves of the same
branch,
In opposite ways we go,
And now opposite lives we know,
Having the same start,
But with a gust of wind we drifted apart

What is it like?
To now be free and fun,
To be known and becoming,
To be a friend to everyone,
What is it like?
To now finally be over there,
To be in the company of those who aren't
self-aware
To be in the company of those who once earned
your jealous stares

Now you're there,
And all I get are whispered hellos
Now you're there
And here I am, a friend no more
I have no envy just contentment
Appreciation for what it is,

I have no anger just love
Appreciation for what it was

For not everything is long-lasting,
This I know
People come and people go
I drink to the memories
And I smile
I see an old friend and wave
It's been a while.

The Greatest Man To Ever Live

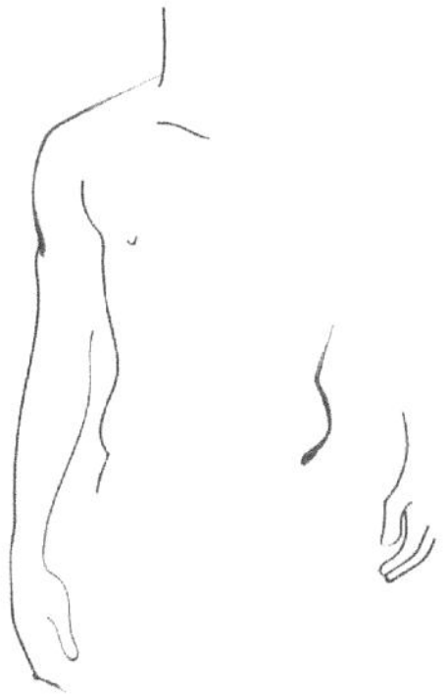

Is it not strange that in one place it is summer
and in another it rains?
That in one life it is joyous and in the other there
is pain?
And is it not even stranger that the removal of
one may cause pain to the other? While the
leaving of one causes joy like no other;

For he sits amongst himself and he cries out,
why?
For why am I being punished aren't I the good
guy?
For he sits and he thinks 'I'm the greatest man to
walk the earth!
Who is she to leave me?
Does she not know my worth?'

And that's why he sits alone,
Because she knew his worth exactly,
His ego was worth more than the finest gold,
And his attitude was ghastly;

Yes she knew his worth very well,
And she knew hers too,
For she was just a simple girl with love in mind,
And life she was trying to get through;

Her rainy days are now like California July's,
She dances her dance without intoxication,
And she laughs till she cries,
A sense of freedom or exhilaration if you will,
For to bandage up the poison is stupidity,
You must suck it out before it kills.

The Delusional Moth

He was a moth and she was fire,
Her beauty like the strongest of drugs,
Robbing him clean of his senses
Higher and higher he went,
On something he believed to be meant,
He felt it in his lungs,
It pulsed through his veins,
He was so enthralled by something that caused
him so much pain.

For she said you fool!
Why do you cry out?
Untiringly I expressed my feelings to you
Day in and day out

So do not blame me!
For I am not some mere fantasy created in your
mind
You so madly listened to your heart
But in reality you chose to be blind

And so the story goes
Somehow the woman is the villain
While she tried to save his heart at her own
expense
She grew tired because he refused to listen!
She tried being kind
She tried being patient
But all of her efforts fell short
He felt like he was owed a reasonable
explanation
But her love could never be forced

He grew indignant as she ignored his desperate
pleas
And thought her heart to be of stone
Please sir, she would say, think whatever you
want
Just as long as you leave me alone!

Pockets Of Happiness

There are these pockets of happiness I
experience in life,
These are the moments I live for
When they come I breathe them in,
Closing my eyes, revering the scent
I engrave them in my mind,
So that when they're gone they're still here.

Morning Time

I cannot rise without it,
Its smoky aroma soothes my soul,
I have succumbed to its power just like those
around me
I said I never would, yet here I am
At the feet of its velvet black skin,
I let its taste awaken me
And now I need it daily
My black coffee.

The Kids On the Block

I've grown weary of the invasive sounds of the
partying kids next door,
They stomp their feet and they raise their voices
and do not slumber until it's past four,
I raise my brow and I tap my foot,
contemplating what I must do
Shall I call the cops?
Shall I take some meds?
What's strong enough to help me sleep through?

On one hand I get it I was once a young lad
Tired of this hopeless domain,
But on the other hand there's fury for such
brazen acts
And the music is driving me insane!

I build up my courage
I zip up my boots
Headed over to give them a piece of my mind

But when I bang on the door and release my
swears
A young man answers who was ever so kind

He smiled hello, invited me in
And asked "Hey man you wanna beer?"
I shook my head no, but then I thought why not?
I haven't had a beer in a year
So he handed me a beer and we talked for a
while,
And I asked, "why must you guys be so loud?"
He said "Young kids like us need to feel music
pulsing through our veins
And that's why we turn up the sound."

So I went to the dance floor and started to see,
How young ones found this so fun
Then they played a song that reminded me of my
youth
And that's when it all begun

I snapped my fingers and I moved my hips,
I howled at the white of the moon
And all of a sudden I felt nineteen again!
The music had me consumed
After this song I swear I'll go home
For this evening wasn't what I had in store
But then they played another

And a beer appeared on my left
And I thought what harm is one more?

Before I knew it, it was far past midnight
I had danced, I had drank, and I had laughed
I told some old jokes, had a few hearts to hearts
And I said "Hey, you kids aren't so bad!"
Then, just when I was about to leave
We were surprised by another knock,
We opened the door thinking it was more
friends,
But were surprised when we discovered the
cops!
The neighbors across apparently called
When they noticed that I went inside
They were worried sick when I didn't come back
out
And assumed that I must've died!

So they ended the night, and put away their
party hats
Before the cops made any arrests
And I coyly snuck out while all my neighbors
watched
Shocked that I was one of the party guests

But before I made it home I felt a light tap
And turned to see the young lad who answered
the door,

He said "We're having a party next weekend,
and we all want you to come,
So you're welcome to join us for more."

I figured I shouldn't, but resist the invite I
couldn't
I nodded my head yes without a second thought
When I laid my head to rest that night I laughed
to myself,
For it was well past four o clock
I'll have a headache tomorrow, and I'm sure I'll
be sick
So I might go visit the doc
When he asks me what happened, I'll laugh to
myself
And blame the cool kids on the block.

The Most Beautiful Rainbow
to Ever Be Seen

I see all people
Like a beautiful rainbow
What a sight to see

Never Laugh Too Quiet

"Hush! Hush!" They would tell me,
You are far too loud,
Your boisterous laugh drowns out your beauty,
And your cackle is drawing a crowd

"I'm so sorry" I would always say,
I don't mean to be this way,
I'm too silly for my own good
That's why I try my best to stay out of the way

My insecurities consume me,
That is why sometimes I do not talk
Since I will go home later in the night
And ask myself why I did not stop

Overanalyzing is an exhausting sport,
That I do not recommend
It's easier to not care so much,
About who likes you and if you'll fit in

Now I laugh even louder,
But attention I do not seek,
I may have a horrendous guffaw
But my only wish is to live free

So let the mockers do what they do best
I'll let them perfect their craft
And when their taunting doesn't reach me
I'll just look at them and laugh.

Exceptionally Forthright

I've never seen myself as exceptionally beautiful
I've never seen myself as exceedingly smart
One thing that I've prided myself on, however
My innate ability to be honest
Some may say callously at times
Though some moments may seem to be the
appropriate setting for pacification of one's
feelings
I could never allow myself to push my pride
aside for such shallow reasonings
More often than not, with strong conviction
I say No
More often than not, with strong conviction
I say I don't want to go
More often than not
I say I don't like it;
And I think that's okay, that these are the things
that I say.

October Falls

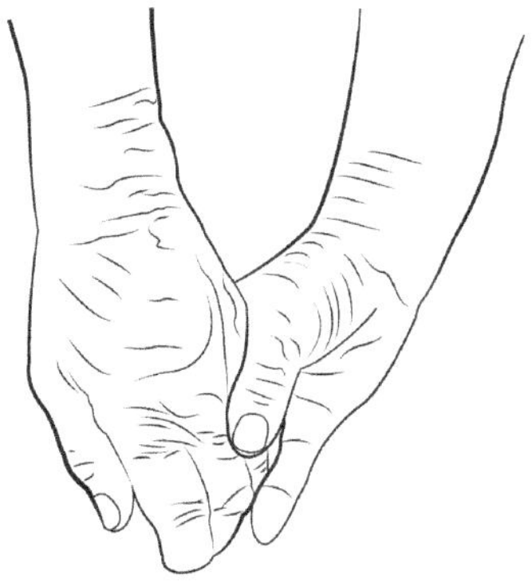

I was born in October
When the leaves would turn brown
I step on them lightly,
yet they still make a sound
Kind of like all the times when you come
around
I try to quiet my heart
But there are brown leaves all around
Fearful of heights,
I've always been afraid to fall down
I have walls built up and you can see them
when I frown
You try to tear those walls down
I try to build them back up
But you sneak in real quick and plant the seeds
of...
Love.

Love Like Sun

You remind me of sun,
So bright it burns when our eyes touch,
Just like the leaves swirl in the breeze,
I'll dance to your song even if it's off-key
You're my worlds gravity,
Holding me down so there's no way to leave

Such an intrusion yet such a delight,
And when we're apart I never feel right
I act like I'm okay but it's only in vain,
Who am I now?
Oh how the seasons change

Being I didn't want to love you,
And I didn't want you here,
And I hate that I love you,
And I hate that I need you near

Darling just hold me,
So I can listen to your heart,
'Cause the sound is like a melody,
You're truly a work of art.

His Deepest Love

Guilt plagues me,
But it is not a trip you've taken me on;
My heart drowns me in regrets,
All from my own doing

It is true, I'm a fool
Incessantly you display the depths of the love
you have for me
But I hide away from them;

My mind cannot comprehend all the good you
see in me
I sabotage myself,
I spray poison all around this beautiful garden
you've given,
Thinking it will turn you away

It's a weird thing the heart does,
Justifying acts our minds would never approve;

I fear that I will one day run out of apologies
And that I will be abandoned here in this
desolate land;

I am battered and bruised,
All from my own doing
I've foolishly believed that my pain was
acceptable because it had no effect on you
But you've loved me so exceptionally, I now
see I have battered you too.

The Man In Blue

If someone were to ask her what she loved most
about him,
She would furrow her brow at the impossibility
of such a question,
For how could she just pick one?

Shall she say
It was the way his integrity seared through his
mighty persona
Shall she say
It was the way he was so famed, yet so often
alone
Shall she say
It was the way he possessed such childlike
curiosity,
Showing it possible for a man to exist
Without the haughtiness of generations before,
Shall she say…
What could she say?

He was seen rugged by fools,
But the ones he trusted he let in,
And inside was warm
He never spoke of futile matters
Perhaps it was because he was anything but a
futile man

Ultimately what intrigued her most,
Was that he was the most perfect combination of
things,
Serious yet humorous,
Tough yet kind,
Gloriously humble,
He was life personified,
And he was everything that you would want a
man to be.

Away With the Stars

There's a skylight in my bathroom,
It's my portal to the stars
Sometimes I look through it and wonder,
Would it be okay if I just drifted away
While everybody slumbered;
I'll take with me the memories,
Memories of family and friends
I'll go to the place of my great escape
Until we meet again.

Assured Expectations

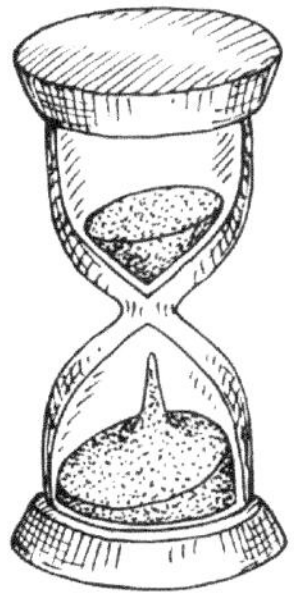

I hope for something beyond these four walls.

To Move Mountains

Up and up I went on this creviced mountain,
Rocky and rough did its edges lay,
Its craggy skin left me bruises
And Its graded land tired me out

I gave it my tears and I spilled out my blood
just so I could remain,
I sweated through my skin trying to fight off my
doubts;
Several times I have been rewarded with grassy
pastures in between
But more times than not I have fallen

I have fallen heavily on defeat time and again,
And when I could no longer stifle my cries, I
would scream out why!
What is the point of this loveless mountain,
And why is it here that all my burdens fall?!

I kept coming back to this rugged land
For there was nowhere else for me to climb,
Then I decided to look up, and that's when I
realized…

For every creviced rock I crawled, I attained
might
For every bruise and scrape, my skin thickened
And for every fall fallen, I was able to go that
much higher the next time

Though this mountain pains me so,
It has only made me stronger
And when I raise my eyes ever so slight
I'm reminded of why I started

So I will not let a fall be the death of me,
And I will not let this mountain have its way!
For I now see the purpose of these rocks that
hurt me
And I find beauty in the bruises that stay.